Royal Style

THE QUEEN MOTHER'S WARDROBE AT THE BOWES MUSEUM

A commemorative book of the Centenary Exhibition June 27 to September 13, 1992 by Joanna Hashagen

CLARENCE HOUSE
S.W. 1

I offer my warmest congratulations to The Bowes Museum on reaching its Centenary.

For the past 100 years my family has had a close association with this magnificent Museum and I have been particularly involved since I became Patron of the Friends in 1962.

I hope that this Exhibition of my dresses which has been arranged to mark the Centenary will be of interest and give pleasure to those who visit your Galleries.

Elizabeth R
The Queen Mother
10th June 1992

Foreword

When we began planning our C ... include in it an event associated ... Museum, Her Majesty Queen El ... be shared by as many people as pos ... The Queen Mother's association ... emblematic. She has been famil ... s in Teesdale, when the 14th Earl ... Bowes domains.

When the Museum reached a critical point in its history, ... shortage of funds were obliging the Trustees to consider transfer of ownership or closure, The Queen Mother added her practical support to a small group of activists who took the name The Friends of the Bowes Museum. Following successful negotiations with Durham County Council, she presided over the formal ceremony of transfer in 1956. A few years later the Friends opened up their membership to any interested persons and The Queen Mother graciously agreed to become Patron. Since then her interest and active support have been constant, not least in Centenary Year.

The special event we wished to organise is this exhibition. It is primarily a homage to The Queen Mother and an expression of gratitude and pleasure for all she has done for The Bowes Museum. It could not have been organised without her support and we are deeply grateful for the thought, time and generosity with which she has responded to our requests to borrow all these items from her wardrobe.

The exhibition also has an underlying purpose, to study how a lady constantly in the public eye, as Queen and Queen Mother, has responded to the symbolic requirements of that role, yet has created an entirely personal style. In the glimpses we have of the planning methods of Sir Norman Hartnell and the unusual chance we have to get close to the clothes themselves, we see what a master couturier he was. And finally, the hats. The wonderful selection presents a group of very imaginative designers and expresses best of all The Queen Mother's zest for life.

The exhibition was the brain-child of the Museum's Costume and Textiles Officer Joanna Hashagen. She and her team in the Textiles Department have created this exhibition with help from colleagues in the Design Department.

This is the first exhibition to be devoted to The Queen Mother's wardrobe. It has been given much financial and practical support by organisations and persons outside the Museum. Several museums have been generous with loans and assistance; the National Portrait Gallery, the Victoria and Albert Museum, the Museum of London, the Court Dress Collection, Kensington Palace, Brighton Art Gallery and Museum and the Museum of Costurme, Bath. Loans from Mr Ian Thomas and Glamis Castle, the family home of the Earls of Strathmore, have provided little known pictorial material. The displays have received generous sponsorship from Glaxo Holdings, plc, Textra Furnishing Fabrics Ltd, Lotus Pearls and the Barnard Castle firms of Waistells, Boothman and Hillery Ltd and J T Young and Sons as well as The North of England Museums Service, The Friends of The Bowes Museum and Durham County Council. Many individual persons have provided information, advice, services and support, particularly Miss Betty Leek, Miss Evelyn Elliott, Miss Gwen Craig and Mrs Sheila Chapman.

This commemorative publication, with its beautiful colour photographs by Jim Kershaw, is a joint venture between The Bowes Museum and The Northern Echo. Their involvement has enabled us to print and distribute a greater number of copies, expanding our aim of sharing the event with as many people as possible.

To all these people and especially to Her Majesty Queen Elizabeth The Queen Mother, I would like to express warmest appreciation and thanks from The Bowes Museum.

Elizabeth Conran
Curator

Lady Elizabeth Bowes-Lyon at the age of 17 by C. Naudin (Strathmore Estates)

The Lady Elizabeth Bowes-Lyon and the Bowes Museum

John Lyon, ninth Earl of Strathmore, initiated the Bowes-Lyon era of family history by his marriage to the heiress Mary Eleanor Bowes in 1767. By the terms of her father's will John Lyon took the name of Bowes. Since 1885 both names have been used and Bowes-Lyon remains the name of the Earls of Strathmore. John Bowes, who with his wife Josephine founded The Bowes Museum in 1869, was the grandson of Mary Eleanor Bowes and the 9th Earl. John Bowes was the illegitimate son of the 10th Earl and so inherited the English lands but not the title. John Bowes's father and The Queen Mother's great great grandfather were brothers. When John Bowes died he left his estate to his cousin's family. In this way after John Bowes's death the English estates were transferred back to the Bowes-Lyon family to be inherited by The Queen Mother's father, the 14th Earl of Strathmore.

Streatlam Castle, two miles from Barnard Castle, was the principal seat of the Bowes family from the 14th century, but John Bowes was the last of the family to make it his principal home. He made major alterations and improvements to the existing 18th century house with new gardens, a pinetum, new stables and an orangery. Streatlam Castle was used for family holidays when Lady Elizabeth Bowes-Lyon (The Queen Mother) was a child, but was sold in 1922. The building was demolished after falling into ruin in 1959. Many of the contents of Streatlam Castle were also sold. However, The Queen Mother retains a portrait of John Bowes at the age of 15 by John Jackson RA which had hung in John Bowes's dining room at Streatlam.

John Bowes had a deep interest in his family history, an interest which is today shared by The Queen Mother. Conscious that he had no heirs, John wrote to his cousin Claude, 13th Earl of Strathmore, with a detailed account of the family papers at Streatlam Castle. He said: 'For if I disappeared, there might be no one to acquaint you with their existence.' Of course, John Bowes was not to know that his family would become linked to royalty and that the retention of the family papers would carry enhanced historical significance. (These papers are now in Durham County Record Office).

Lady Elizabeth Bowes-Lyon grew up in the Strathmore's ancestral home of Glamis Castle in Scotland. During her childhood visits to the Strathmore estate in Teesdale she must have visited her relative's museum. She has continued to visit The Bowes Museum throughout her life. Her interest is both deep and personal. It is known that she encourages members of her family to visit, enjoy and share its pleasures.

In 1976 The Queen Mother opened the Queen Elizabeth Gallery of Costume. In her address she said: 'The creation of the Costume Gallery marks a further landmark – and a most imaginative one – in the many exciting developments of recent years. This new venture is particularly opportune for, during the lifetime of all of us here today, there has been a change in outlook and circumstance which it is sometimes hard to realise. Nothing more vividly reflects the habits and inclinations of our forebears than the clothes they wore;

Photo C – The Duchess of York in Teesdale, County Durham in 1925. This is a snap by an amateur photographer outside Laithkirk church. The Duchess would have been staying on the Earl of Strathmore's estate in Teesdale. During her stay she had visited the centenary celebrations of Darlington Railway (Parkin Raine)

THE EARLS OF STRATHMORE

Her Majesty the Queen Mother's father was Claude George (1865-1944) 14th Earl
grandfather Claude (1824-1904) 13th Earl
Great grandfather Thomas George (1801-1834) did not live to succeed to the title
Great-great grandfather Thomas (1773-1847) 11th Earl
Great-great-great grandfather John Lyon (1737-1776) 9th Earl
The 9th Earl was the grandfather of The Bowes Museum co-founder John Bowes and was the Queen Mother's great-great-great grandfather

THE GENERATIONS AND THE EARLS

John Lyon 9th Earl of Strathmore
m. Mary Eleanor Bowes 1767

John (Lyon Bowes) (1769-1820) **m.** Mary Miller | Thomas (1775-1846) 11th Earl **m.** Mary Elizabeth Carpenter | George | Dau | Dau

John Bowes (1811-1885) | Thomas George (1801-1834) **m.** Charlotte Grinstead | Dau

S | Thomas George (1822-1865) 12th Earl | Claude (1824-1904) 13th Earl | Dau

Claude George (1855-1944) 14th Earl | S | S | S

Patrick (1884-1949) 15th Earl | S | S | S | Michael Claude Hamilton (1893-1953) | David | Dau | Dau | Dau | Elizabeth Angela Marguerite (1900- Her Majesty The Queen Mother

Timothy (1949-1972) 16th Earl | Fergus Michael Claude (1972-) 17th Earl

Children not named appear as s (son) or dau (daughter). Sons appear first, irrespective of their date of birth

their beauty and workmanship is often a delight to behold and their design recalls more gracious and leisured days.'

It is hoped that through this book and exhibition the beauty and workmanship of The Queen Mother's wardrobe can be appreciated and that through these clothes the personality of The Queen Mother is captured.

Joanna Hashagen

Above – One of a series of photographs taken during a shooting party on the Glamis Estate in 1924 or 1925. This one shows the 14th Earl of Strathmore and his daughters, The Duchess of York and Lady Rose Bowes-Lyon. The Duchess of York is wearing a knitted silk suit bound with silk braid by Zyrot and a suede hat first worn for her honeymoon at Polesden Lacey, Surrey, the previous year. The shooting party included the Prince of Wales, the Duke of York and members of the Strathmore family (Strathmore Estates)

Opposite page, left – The Hon. Elizabeth Bowes-Lyon with her younger brother David photographed by Speaight, 1904 (Strathmore Estates)

Opposite page, right – The Bowes Museum, Barnard Castle

Duchess

When Lady Elizabeth Bowes-Lyon married Prince Albert, Duke of York, on April 26 1923, she came to the forefront of public life and clothes were no longer private affairs. The Court dressmaker, Madame Handley Seymour of New Bond Street, created the medieval style wedding gown. The Graphic described it at the time as 'inspired by Italy of the fourteenth century............of ivory chiffon mousmé, a very new watered satin-faced georgette'.

The bride's trousseau was in subtle colours, in soft, fashionable fabrics of the day like crêpe-de-chine, often adorned with furs. The slight figure of the Duchess suited the simple straight line of the 1920's style. Most of the trousseau was by Handley Seymour, with additions by Jays and hats by Zyrot et Cie.

When the Duchess of York became Queen Elizabeth she remained loyal to Mrs Handley Seymour for her Coronation gown in 1937, which had to be completed in record time following the abdication. The embroidery encompassed the emblems of England, Ireland, Scotland, Wales, Canada, New Zealand and Australia. The purple velvet robe carried the same national emblems in gold thread and was made by Ede and Ravenscroft, Court robe makers. The embroidery was designed and worked by The Royal School of Needlework.

The Coronation Maids of Honour holding up the Coronation robe of purple velvet embroidered in gold thread. It is almost 18ft long. Norman Hartnell designed the dresses worn by the maids of honour. Photograph by Hay Wrightson 1937. (National Portrait Gallery)

nd Queen

The wedding dress of silk chiffon moiré, the front decorated with bands of silver lamé embroidered with seed pearls, iridescent white beads and silver thread. The loose fitting bodice has a low, square neckline and short sleeves. A short train is pleated into the back waistband. By Handley Seymour.

Lady Elizabeth Bowes Lyon leaving her family home at 17 Bruton Street, Mayfair, for her wedding. Queen Mary loaned the veil which was worn with a wreath of myrtle leaves with white roses and orange blossom above each ear.

For going away, the Duchess of York wore an ensemble which consisted of a dress and jacket and matching coat. The dress and jacket of mushroom coloured silk crêpe romaine, pictured left – is machine embroidered all over with a Chinese-style design of flowers and small buildings. The dress is low-waisted and of an intricate construction with a wrap-over tiered skirt. The matching jacket has a beaded belt attached to the back creating blouson effect behind, leaving the open fronts of the jacket, which are weighted, to fall free.

The Duchess of York with the Duke of York and her parents the Earl and Countess of Strathmore at Glamis Castle, 1924. The occasion was a garden party for which the Duchess wore her going-away outfit (Strathmore Estates)

Detail of the outfit shows the belt of the jacket decorated with shell-like and painted beads, the decoration on the sleeve and the embroidery of the dress.

Left: back view of the matching coat in a heavier silk crêpe. It has applied circles of ruched fabric enlivening a very simple cut, typical of the 1920s. By Handley Seymour.

The back view of the dress worn for the Coronation of George VI, May, 1937, by Handley Seymour. It is satin embroidered with gold thread, diamanté and spangles with roses, thistles, shamrocks, leeks, lotus, maple leaves and mimosa – the national emblems. It has short satin sleeves and long, hanging sleeves of net with needlepoint lace (Point de gaze). The bias-cut gown sweeps into a short train. (The property of HM Queen Elizabeth The Queen Mother held on deposit by The Museum of London. Photograph The Museum of London)

The White

The first important event of the new reign was a State visit to France in 1938. Norman Hartnell was invited to create the Queen's wardrobe for the visit.
George V1 had shown Hartnell Winterhalter's portraits of Eugenie of France and Elizabeth of Austria wearing crinolines by Worth, suggesting they were a suitably regal image for his Queen. The success of the play 'Victoria Regina' shown on the London stage in 1937, in which the crinoline featured, may also have strengthened Hartnell's resolve to revive the crinoline for the Queen. Thirty designs were accepted and the colours of the fabrics chosen, but just before the final fittings the Queen's mother, the Countess of Strathmore, died and the Court went into mourning. Black or purple seemed totally inappropriate for July and may have offended the French. Hartnell's solution was to adopt a less well known mourning colour – white. Within two weeks all the dresses were remade in white. They caused a sensation in the French Press; Paris was enchanted by the romantic designs of beautiful, diaphanous fabrics. Hartnell was awarded the Palms of an Officer of the Academie Francaise and credited with reintroducing the crinoline to Paris. HM Queen Elizabeth The Queen Mother has lent three of the five principal dresses worn for this famous state visit to the exhibition.

Dress worn for the garden party at Bagatelle on the State Visit to France July 1938. Described by Hartnell as 'of the finest cobweb lace and tulle', it has a low waisted tiered skirt with draped bodice and short sleeves trimmed with a spray of flowers at the waist. It was worn with a broad brimmed hat trimmed with osprey feathers and a matching lace parasol. (On loan from H.M. The Queen Mother to The Royal Pavilion Brighton Museum and Art Gallery).

Wardrobe

Dress of silk organdie embroidered all over with open work embroidery worn for a luncheon held in la Galerie des Glaces (Hall of Mirrors) at the Palace of Versailles. It was worn with a leghorn hat trimmed with a black velvet ribbon. The bodice has a 'V' neckline and short sleeves, the skirt is tiered, worn with georgette and net underskirts, their hems trimmed with lace. Detail from skirt showing the 'broderie anglaise' flowers and the transparency of the silk organdie.

Portrait of H.M. Queen Elizabeth The Queen Mother by Sir Gerald Kelly c. 1938. Oil study showing Her Majesty wearing the evening dress worn for the Gala Performance at the Paris Opera during the 1938 state visit with the Most Noble Order of the Garter on her left arm and the Garter sash. (By courtesy of the National Portrait Gallery)

The evening dress worn for the Gala performance at the Paris Opera during the 1938 state visit. A satin crinoline, worn with a hooped petticoat, trimmed with lace, embroidered with silver thread, sequins and diamanté. The skirt has three tiers of pleated satin swags edged with lace and the dress is trimmed with sprays of white velvet camelias.

Hartnell and Beaton

Cecil Beaton first photographed The Queen in 1939 wearing dresses from the white wardrobe. He transformed her into a fairytale Queen dressed in Hartnell's bespangled crinolines. Together Beaton and Hartnell established a new romantic image for the monarchy. In 1948 Beaton returned to this Victorian image but presented The Queen as an elegant, mature woman wearing a magnificent black velvet crinoline. It was Beaton's idea to photograph The Queen in unaccustomed black and Hartnell made the costume specially for this photographic session.

The fitted bodice has a draped yoke worn off the shoulder. The very full three-tiered skirt has a broad double band of piping at each gathered tier which provides the support for the fullness. There was no hooped petticoat with this dress.

For the photographic portrait the dress was set off by Queen Victoria's diamond tassle brooch, two diamond necklaces, a bracelet and the 'Indian' tiara. Beaton often posed The Queen against grand painted backdrops to create pastiches of paintings by Winterhalter. (Camera Press)

Sir Norman Hartnell was one of the great British couturiers, famous above all for having dressed royalty so successfully. He understood perfectly the requirements of Royal dressing; that each outfit had to be suitable for its function as well as being glamorous and dramatic. He enjoyed a special relationship with The Queen Mother, as did Beaton, until his death in 1979. Her Majesty was loyal to him from 1938 and many of his early designs for outfits for her are included in the exhibition. They show sophisticated, fashionable styles for the new Queen. Today The Queen Mother continues to buy her clothes exclusively from the House of Hartnell.

Stately Elegance

Queen Elizabeth The Queen Mother's evening gowns for formal and state occasions are a triumph of regal splendour. Hartnell's mastery in creating heavily embroidered and bejewelled designs on lustrous satins are a match for the priceless royal jewels worn with them.

Above – Detail from the front of the skirt showing the beaded decoration of silver-gilt metal spangles, bugle beads and rhinestones and mock citrines in claw settings.

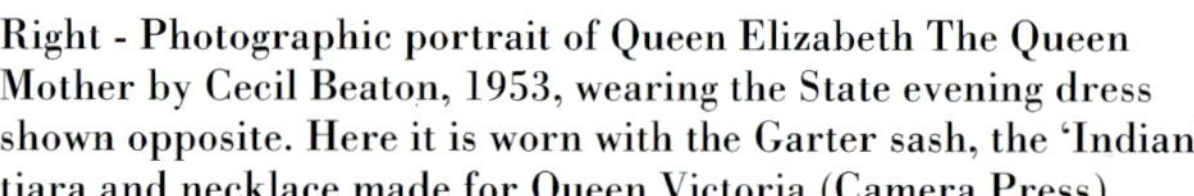

Right - Photographic portrait of Queen Elizabeth The Queen Mother by Cecil Beaton, 1953, wearing the State evening dress shown opposite. Here it is worn with the Garter sash, the 'Indian' tiara and necklace made for Queen Victoria (Camera Press).

Pictured opposite – State evening dress of Duchesse satin with beaded decoration. The full circular skirt was worn with hooped petticoat. Worn for a gala performance of Sadler's Wells Ballet at Covent Garden, 1950. (On loan from HM Queen Elizabeth The Queen Mother to The Court Dress Collection, Kensington Palace).

The Queen Mother has continued to wear the same style of evening dress; sleeveless with low, often off-the-shoulder neckline and deep cape collars covering the top of the arms and with full crinoline skirts. One exception was the dress with red beaded decoration which has a straight skirt. Detail opposite.

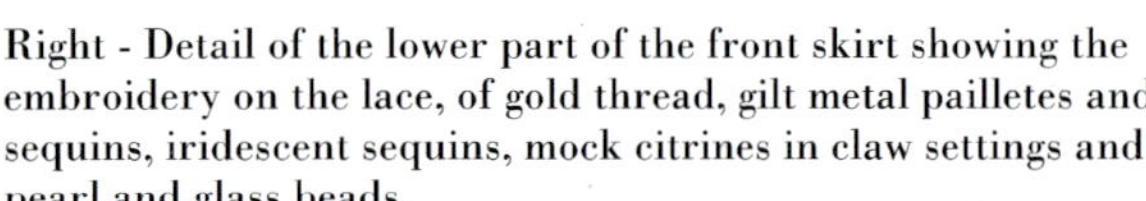

Right - Detail of the lower part of the front skirt showing the embroidery on the lace, of gold thread, gilt metal pailletes and sequins, iridescent sequins, mock citrines in claw settings and pearl and glass beads.

Right – Evening dress of Duchesse satin overlaid with lace, the lace design outlined in gold thread and beaded. Worn with a hooped petticoat. (On long loan from HM Queen Elizabeth The Queen Mother to The Bowes Museum).

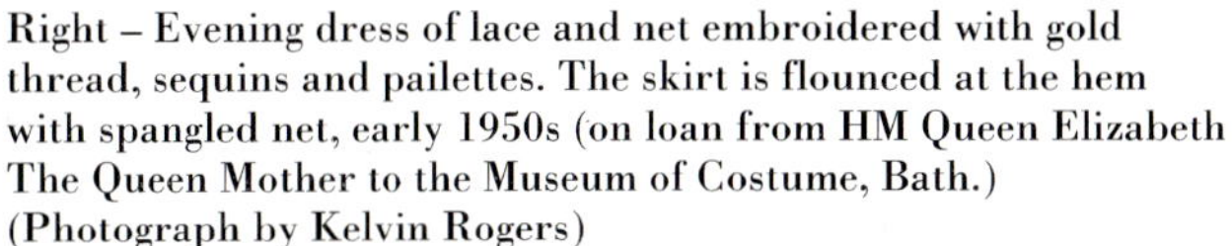

Right – Evening dress of lace and net embroidered with gold thread, sequins and pailettes. The skirt is flounced at the hem with spangled net, early 1950s (on loan from HM Queen Elizabeth The Queen Mother to the Museum of Costume, Bath.) (Photograph by Kelvin Rogers)
Above – Detail of the embroidered design of flower heads in white and blue beads, brilliant pailettes and sequins from a state evening dress, 1950. (Donated by HM Queen Elizabeth The Queen Mother to the Victoria and Albert Museum, loaned by the Trustees of the Victoria and Albert Museum). (Photograph, the Victoria and Albert Museum.)
Below – Border of bead embroidery from the front hem of the full length evening dress of ivory satin. It has a straight skirt with an open overskirt faced with ruby red satin. The beading includes diamanté and sequins and mock rhinestones and rubies in claw settings. Late 1960s, early 1970s.

Family Celebrations

This group of dresses was personally selected by Queen Elizabeth The Queen Mother for the exhibition. She has chosen family celebrations of christenings and weddings which will hold very special memories for her. They are also perhaps the clothes which she particularly enjoyed wearing. Rather than the stiff formal gowns worn for state occasions, she has chosen soft, luxuriant fabrics in silver, bronze and gold. They are still grand and dignified, but the soft drapery is more feminine and reflects the warmth of her personality. Hartnell skilfully used the fabrics to best effect creating flattering and comfortable styles. Most successful are the softly pleated cross-over bodices and the draped wrap-over skirts which provide extra fabric when she is sitting down. A favourite detail was a bow or sash at the side of the waist.

These features typify the style of Her Majesty's dresses of the 1940s and 1950s. The dress of bronze lamé worn for Princess Anne's christening is almost identical to the dress worn for Prince Charles's christening in 1948, also of bronze lamé. It is also similar to the full length dress of gold and apricot lamé worn for the wedding of Princess Elizabeth in 1947.

Right – A dress of bronze lamé with cross-over bodice, padded shoulders, three-quarter length sleeves and draped skirt with sash belt worn for the christening of Princess Anne on October 21, 1950. below. It was worn with a feather trimmed hat.

Above – Dress of gold and silver lamé with a matching stole trimmed with mink worn for Princess Margaret's wedding on May 10, 1960 at Westminster Abbey. The dress is cleverly styled with diagonal tucks on the bodice and skirt to create an elegant and slender line. The draped stole adds interest when seen from the back.

Left – Dress and matching coat of silver tissue lace edged with grey-blue net worn for Princess Alexandra's wedding on April 24, 1963 at Westminster Abbey. It was worn with a feather-trimmed hat.

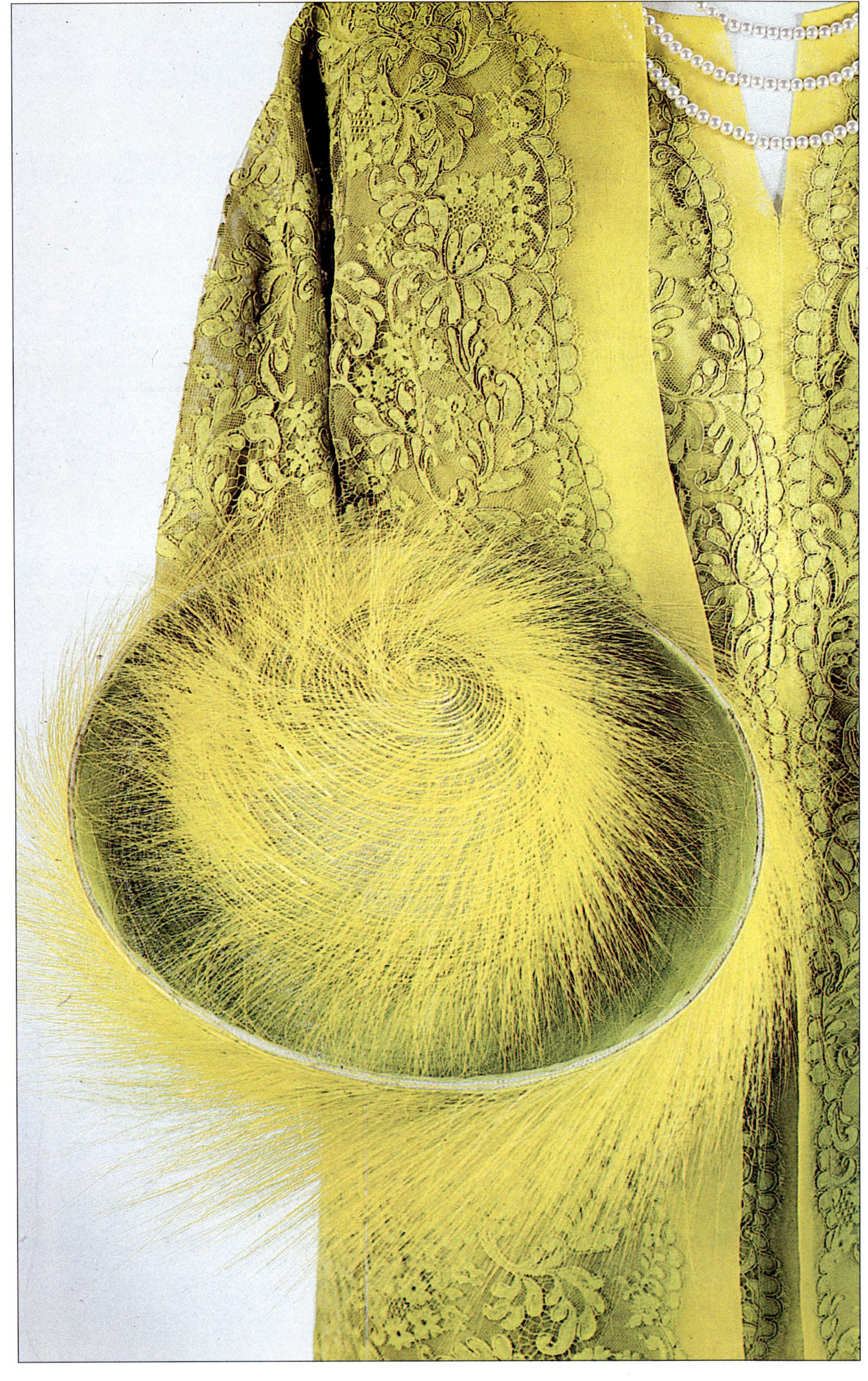

Royal Engagements

The wide range of royal engagements require differing styles, colours and fabrics.Colour may be governed by the wearing of foreign orders and decorations or the presence of military uniform. The choice of lime green for the Investiture of the Prince of Wales in direct contrast to red tunics of the Guards is a stunning example.
The velvet coat, dress and hat is the type of outfit worn for more informal official visits, for example, to universities to confer degrees. These simple, loose fitting coats with three quarter length sleeves, often fur trimmed, have become a recognisable and successful formula.

The Investiture of the Prince of Wales, Caernarvon 1969. Here it would seem that the royal ladies have discussed colours beforehand although it is said that this is not always the case! (Hulton Picture Company).

Above – Dress and coat of floral printed silk overlaid with silk chiffon printed in the same design worn for Ascot in 1973. Teamed with an unusually large and full brimmed hat of layers of orange net by Rudolf for an occasion when hats are expected to be frivolous. This outfit was chosen by The Queen Mother to represent her style of dress for Royal Ascot.

Left – Coat of brown velvet with dress of silk chiffon with a woven check in gold thread. The dress was made in 1973. The hat of matching gold fabric and feathers is by Rudolf.

Opposite page – Dress and coat of lace lined and edged in silk chiffon with matching hat of osprey by Simone Mirman, worn for the Investiture of the Princes of Wales, Caernarvon on July 1, 1969. The dress has floating chiffon panels from a curved yoke. The striking lime green colour, perhaps influenced by the bright colours of the 1960s, is a perfect choice for being visible from a distance by a large crowd.

Chiffon

The Queen Mother has developed a unique style of dress. The floating chiffons and extravagant hats have become her version of Royal style. It is instantly recognisable as hers, while reflecting her relaxed demeanour and warm personality.
Her favourite colours are clear pastel shades, in particular blues and lilacs. These pretty colours work well with her choice of fabrics. The Queen Mother loves soft silks. These delicate lightweight silks and chiffons are extremely flattering when draped and layered. Further softness is sometimes created with fur and feather trimmings. The floating chiffon panels and the straight line of the coats help to make her appear taller. The creation of layers with matching coats softens the line, but is also very practical. Often a dress will have both a matching chiffon coat and one in a heavier weight silk. In this way layers can be removed or added according to the weather.
Since Norman Hartnell's death, the vendeuse, Evelyn Elliott has orchestrated the Queen Mother's wardrobe. 'Miss Evelyn' has been at Hartnell's for 40 years and has been going to Clarence House for 30. The process begins with the submission of sketches and swatches of fabric from which The Queen Mother makes her choice. There follows a series of fittings, at three to four week intervals. In the past, Hartnell was given a detailed itinerary by The Queen Mother so that he could design specifically for each function. These days the outfits are no longer designed for particular occasions.

Above – Dress and coat of silk chiffon printed in a swirling design, 1970. The bodice and the waist of the dress are softly draped in cross-over panels in contrast to the simplicity of the coat. Worn with a hat of pointed chiffon petals, each point trimmed with a small flower bud, by Simone Mirman, 1970. The hint of a modern late 1960s abstract pattern has been softened by the 'sweet pea' colours.
Worn for her birthday in August 1970 and in June of that year for an agricultural show with a different flower petal hat. Seen here with three of her grandchildren, Lady Sarah Armstrong-Jones, Prince Edward and Viscount Linley, in the garden of Clarence House (Hulton Picture Company)

and Silk

Left – Dress and coat of printed floral silk. Coat has semi-circular cape sleeves attached at the top shoulder only so that they float freely. This was worn with a white straw hat with upturned brim and blue veil trimmed with a pink rose by Rudolf.
Above – The outfit was worn to open The Queen Elizabeth Gallery of Costume at The Bowes Museum in 1976. (Gordon Coates)

Right– Dress and coat of printed silk chiffon. A simple, sleeveless dress with a low, round collar and matching belt. Worn with a matching hat trimmed with cornflowers by Rudolf, 1977. It was chosen by The Queen Mother for the exhibition to represent this type of favourite outfit.

Below – Dress of silk overlaid with silk chiffon, with matching chiffon scarf, worn for the Investiture of Norman Hartnell in 1977. The dress was made up in the Hartnell workrooms in Norman Hartnell's favourite shade of blue, but without his knowing of its creation. In this way The Queen Mother was able to both surprise and please him at the moment he was knighted.

Left –Dress of lilac silk chiffon with two floating panels falling from a curved back yoke to hem with matching osprey trimmed hat by Rudolf worn for Thanksgiving Service at St Paul's Cathedral for The Queen Mother's 80th birthday.

Above – The Queen Mother and members of her family in the White Drawing Room at Buckingham Palace after the Thanksgiving Service, July 15, 1980. (Hulton Picture Company)

Putting on the Style

Hats allow an instant and clear statement for the wearer. Royal hats can and do stand out from the crowd. They are unique and different. The Queen Mother's hats are simply stunning. There is great variety; sometimes they are frivolous and fun, in bright colours and with eye catching trimmings. The hats are lively and movement is created by feathers and trimmings. A motif, such as an acorn, is noticeable and may be linked to a mood or specific occasion. The joie de vivre of The Queen Mother is captured well in many of these wonderful creations. Wearing these beautiful hats must have given as much pleasure to the wearer as to those who observe. They are structures which have their own sculptural form and thus stand up in their own right, more so than the dresses. These hats are a tribute to the milliner's art and skill.

Queen Elizabeth The Queen Mother's first milliner was a Dane, Aage Thaarup. He began making hats for her in the 1930s when she was the Duchess of York.

After 1953 Hartnell chose a French milliner, Madame Claude Saint-Cyr, who would fly across from Paris to create hats to suit his designs. Another French milliner, Jean Barthet, is also represented. By 1965 he was generally considered to be the foremost milliner in France. In 1960 The Queen Mother began to buy hats from Simone Mirman, a French woman who set up her

Above: Yellow and white flowers and feather fronds, by Rudolf, 1974.

Above: Blue feather with ostrich feather pom-pom at side by Rudolf, 1973. Worn for the photograph by Norman Parkinson and used on British postage stamp, 1975.

own establishment in London in 1947.
In 1969 Norman Hartnell introduced The Queen Mother to the milliner Rudolf, an exiled Czech nobleman, who from the early 1970s seems to have made the majority of her hats. Since his death in 1980 his partner Joy Quested-Nowell has continued to make The Queen Mother's hats under the Rudolf label.
The Australian Frederick Fox is milliner by appointment to Her Majesty Queen Elizabeth II but sometimes makes hats for The Queen Mother as does Ian Thomas, one of the Queen's couturiers.
Each hat is designed for a specific Hartnell outfit and often two different styles of hat are produced for each outfit to help ring the changes. They often have a small swatch of the dress fabric attached inside so that they can be matched easily. Every hat has two hat pins covered with matching fabric to ensure that the hats stay firmly in place.

Above: Silk flowers in many colours, by Simone Mirman.

Right: Pink osprey with floral printed silk in turban style, by Rudolf.

Above: Pink net with white dots, by Simone Mirman.

Above: Blue silk rose, by Simone Mirman.

Above: Beige osprey feather and straw, by Simone Mirman. Similar to the one worn for Princess Margaret's wedding.

Left: Blue and white rose petal with blue veil, by Rudolf. The Queen Mother is pictured wearing this hat for a visit to The Bowes Museum in 1982. This hat was also worn for Ascot.

Right - Blue wool felt with brim, with pheasant feathers by Frederick Fox, 1980s.

Centre left - Yellow silk with upturned brim, the crown forming four points like an opening flower bud, trimmed with chiffon and silk flowers, by Rudolf.

Centre right - Wool jersey green, red and cream with woollen pom-pom by Rudolf.

Bottom left - Pleated purple silk with brim, veil and silk flowers by Rudolf.

Bottom right - Green silk trimmed with acorns and brown veil, by Rudolf 1977.

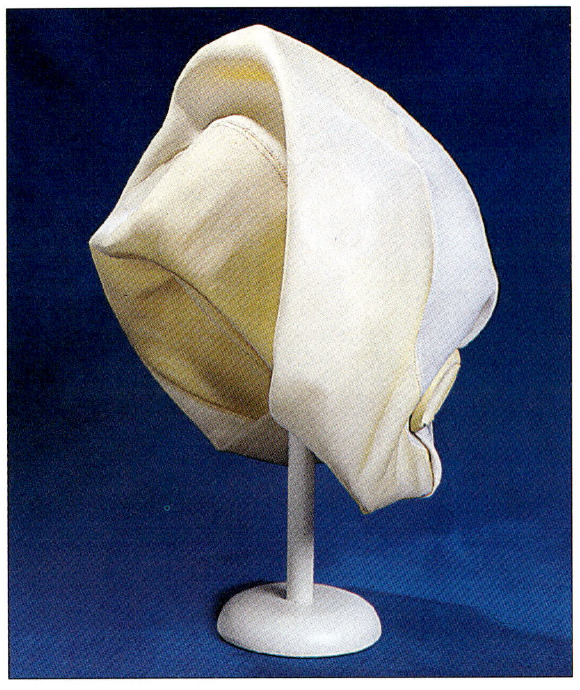

Top left - Lemon and cream silk organza, by Rudolf.

Top right - Green wool velour with feathers and veil, by Simone Mirman.

Centre left - Pale green silk jersey with feathers by Jean Barthet, Paris, 1950s.

Centre right - Interwoven strips of purple silk and ostrich feather fronds, by Claude Saint-Cyr, Paris, 1960s.

Left - Blue cornflowers on chiffon by Simone Mirman.

The Queen Mother has recently returned to the Breton style of brimmed hats with the addition of a veil following the success of those by Thaarup in the 1940s. This style of brim allows the full face of The Queen Mother to be seen, which she clearly intends. In the 1950s the hats tended to be smaller and closer to the head, worn without brims, but by the 1960s they became more extravagant with Simone Mirman's bold flowery or osprey feather creations. The successful association with Rudolf produced an array of inventive designs for the 1970s. The hats in the exhibition by Simone Mirman date mainly from the late 1960s and those by Rudolf were worn in the 1970s and early 1980s.
For Royalty the hat is a symbol of high position; for The Queen Mother it is also an expression of her ebullience and enjoyment of life.

Above – Peach silk with matching silk roses and green veil, by Rudolf.

Top right – White straw and blue net with upturned brim and veil, trimmed wth blue silk roses by Rudolf, 1982. This hat was worn for Prince William's christening on August 4, 1982 - The Queen Mother's birthday. Pictured on opposite page.

Right, centre – Apple blossom with woven green straw bands, 1972 by Ian Thomas, London.

Right – Blue, turquoise and white printed silk with blue veil by Rudolf, 1975. This hat was worn for a visit to Holwick in Teesdale, July, 1975, pictured opposite page. She was visiting Holwick Lodge, the Earl of Strathmore's hunting lodge, and also attended the Museum Association conference at Beamish Museum and opened the Timothy Hackworth Museum in Shildon.

29

Above - Her Majesty Queen Elizabeth The Queen Mother inspecting officer cadets at Catterick Garrison, North Yorkshire, in 1940. Note the jaunty side angle of her hat, typical of Thaarup's designs of the 1940s. It is decorated with a jewelled thistle badge given to her by The King.

Left - HM Queen Elizabeth the Queen Mother on Ripon station, April 8, 1953. She is wearing black, in mourning for Queen Mary who had died in March.

The Queen Mother in the North

Above left - The Duke and Duchess of York at the opening of Glamis pit owned by John Bowes and Partners Ltd at Kibblesworth, County Durham, on July 29, 1936 (Durham County Record Office and the Earl of Strathmore)

Above - At the Duchess's request, the Royal Party descended onto the coal face after donning protective clothing.

Left - The Queen Mother is helped out of her coat on arrival at the Royal Show in Newcastle, July, 1962. It shows a contrast in style of hats.

Above left - A visit to Catterick Garrison in October, 1968. The Queen Mother is wearing a wool coat, fur-trimmed, in her favourite style, with a feather hat. Although fashions change, The Queen Mother presents a consistent and dignified image.

Above - The Queen Mother looking radiant in the Royal Box of The Georgian Theatre, Richmond, North Yorkshire in June, 1969. She is wearing a beaded evening dress with a full length crinoline skirt and a fur wrap.

Left - The Queen Mother meeting the crowds on a visit to Durham, November, 1980, wearing one of her favourite styles of brimmed hat.

Below - A proud moment at Catterick Garrison in June 1972. The Queen Mother is wearing a hat of feather and ostrich feather fronds and her favourite length of sleeve.

Above - The Queen Mother enjoying a performance of The SIlver Swan, an 18th century life-size mechanical swan of silver which performs daily at The Bowes Museum. She is wearing a pink flower petal hat. The occasion was the centenary of the founding of The Bowes Museum in June, 1969. Josephine Bowes laid the first stone in 1869, but the museum did not open to the public until June 10, 1892.

Right - Visit by Her Majesty Queen Elizabeth The Queen Mother on the occasion of the formal transfer of The Bowes Museum to Durham County Council, November 1, 1956. The velvet coat, of a deep violet blue, is very similar to the one illustrated on Page 19. The small neat hat is decorated with violets.

Lenders

Her Majesty Queen Elizabeth The Queen Mother
The Board of Trustees of the National Portrait Gallery, London
Strathmore Estates
Ian Thomas, LVO
The Board of Trustees of the Victoria and Albert Museum, London.
The following museums facilitated the loan of dresses on loan to them from HM Queen Elizabeth the Queen Mother: The Museum of Costume, Bath; The Royal Pavilion Brighton Art Gallery and Museum; the State Apartments and Court Dress Collection, Kensington Palace; The Museum of London, with thanks to their curators of costume.

Exhibition sponsors

Glaxo Holdings plc, Textra Furnishing Fabrics Ltd and North of England Newspapers; with assistance from J. Barbour and Sons Ltd, Lotus Pearls and the Barnard Castle firms of Waistells, Boothman and Hillery Ltd and J.T. Young and Sons. The exhibition has been supported by The North of England Museums Service, The Friends of the Bowes Museum and Durham County Council.

Acknowledgements

We are most grateful to Her Majesty's dresser Miss Betty Leek and the vendeuse from Hartnell, Miss Evelyn Elliott, who have been most helpful with information and advice; Ian Thomas LVO and Mr Silverman of Hartnell Ltd for useful information.
Special thanks are due to; Sue Kendrew, Publications Editor of The Northern Echo; Alastair Gilmour, Graphic Designer of The Northern Echo and Gwen Craig at Textra. Thanks are also due to Terence Pepper (The National Portrait Gallery) Lt Col Cardwell-Moore MBE (Strathmore Estate) Jennifer Gill (Durham County Records Office) for help with photographs and Sheila Chapman (North of England Museums Service) for assistance with fund-raising.

Photography

Colour photographs: Jim Kershaw, unless otherwise credited
Monochrome: From the Photographic Library of North of England Newspapers Ltd, unless otherwise credited.
Back cover: Photograph by Anthony Crickmay, a portrait for The Queen Mother's 90th birthday.
Front cover: Photographic portrait of Queen Elizabeth The Queen Mother by Cecil Beaton, 1953 (Camera Press)

The Bowes Museum is part of the Arts, Libraries and Museums Department of Durham County Council. It is in Barnard Castle, County Durham, four miles from Bowes (A66), 12 miles from Scotch Corner (A66/A1), 17 miles from Darlington (A67) and 26 miles from Durham (A688/B6074/A167). It is open daily all the year round except near Christmas. An information leaflet and publications list may be otained from The Bowes Museum, Barnard Castle, County Durham DL12 8NP. Tel 0833 690606.

The Northern Echo, Priestgate, Darlington
Co. Durham DL3 1NF. Tel 0325 381313.